IF I HAD A

HORSE

How Different Life Would Be

IF I HAD A
HORSE

How Different Life Would Be

BY MELISSA SOVEY-NELSON

PHOTOGRAPHS BY MARK J. BARRETT

Willow Creek Press

Photographs © Mark J. Barrett

Published by Willow Creek Press,
P.O. Box 147, Minocqua, Wisconsin 54548

Editor: Andrea Donner
Design: Jackie Cairns-Barrett

Library of Congress Cataloging-in-Publication Data

Sovey-Nelson, Melissa.
    If I had a horse : how different life would be / by Melissa Sovey-Nelson ;
photography by Mark Barrett.
        p. cm.
    ISBN 1-57223-884-4 (hardcover : alk. paper)
    1. Horses. 2. Quotations, English. I. Title.
    SF301.S68 2004
    636.1--dc22
                                    2004002256

Printed in Canada

For Michael, Parker, and Drew

Thank you, Crni

CONTENTS

*Riding a horse is not a gentle hobby, to be
picked up and laid down like a game of solitaire.
It is a grand passion. It seizes a person whole
and, once it has done so, he will have to accept
that his life will be radically changed.*

— Ralph Waldo Emerson

10   *If I Had A Horse*

INTRODUCTION

For a girl smitten with horses, mythologies come alive in storybooks and in precious plastic replicas placed with care on bedroom shelves. Stories of wild mustangs leaping from cliffs rather than face capture, tales of equine heroes who sacrificed their lives for the person who loved them, all become part and parcel of the captivation that occurs once the horse runs freely through the bloodstream.

Hopefully, if this is you, you have not been discouraged in your dreaming. Many of the fantasies young girls have about horses are not only full of the potential that the horse/woman relationship promises, but are also tremendous symbols for personal growth in leadership, courage, and empowerment.

One of the earliest religious disappointments in a young girl's life devolves upon her unanswered prayer for a horse.

– Phyllis Theroux

Why does this animal engage the female heart so completely? Perhaps it is because the horse is not the captor of our hearts at all, but the messenger of commandeering our own lives, truly setting us free.

In the company of a horse, already perfect in his nature, we discover our own authenticities. We form a trusting relationship not by controlling, but by earning our place as a fit leader while remaining ever the student. If we know that a horse needs us to be the alpha mare in order to establish faith and willingness, we must be willing to understand what this may require from us as well. It is often a humbling experience, where we are confronted with fear, self-doubt or buried emotions.

But it is also a rewarding place that finely tunes natural intuition and compassion, empowering and validating the strength that is the female spirit.

I was not one of those horse-loving girls, despite the fact that I spent my preadolescent days on a farm. We had chickens and ducks, goats, a lovely pig, an assortment of dogs and cats and a couple of horses. My mother is an avid horse lover; my older sister would become an accomplished and highly respected horse trainer and equestrian, yet I spent my days with my younger sisters exploring the outdoors, climbing trees and building forts. Horses were not calling to me, yet.

When we moved to northern Wisconsin many years later, my first friends were horsewomen. My children were all away at school and I had a newfound freedom with my days. I accepted an invitation to a day-long dressage clinic on a warm August Sunday not knowing quite what to expect.

I was mesmerized by both the riders and the horses; their elegant and often seamless movements looked like kinetic poetry. I could barely detect the subtle communication that I knew had to exist in order for woman and horse to appear so coalesced. By the end of the evening a new journey was beginning for me.

I began dressage lessons, borrowing the proper attire and riding a school horse that I immediately fell in love with. While respectful of his size and power, I was not afraid — I was enchanted. I admired his graciousness and patience. Meticulous by nature, I was nevertheless delighted with the pungently muddy and hairy interior of my car. Between lessons I was yearning for the next ride, often horseback in my dreams.

It wasn't long before I had a horse of my own, a spirited half Arabian named Crni. What a pair we made, both green but anxious to learn. I like to think that we continue growing together, but the truth is that he has far more to teach me than I him.

Reading everything I could get my hands on, watching videos and familiarizing myself with terminology, I felt I was equipping myself with all the necessary tools to become the horsewoman I wanted to be. Little did I realize at the time, that the horse himself would provide my finest education in horsemanship and "humanship," and that what was emerging from our relationship had little to do with reading books or accumulating facts.

As much as I looked forward to riding, I would often become extremely nervous as I approached the barn, even fearful at times. My instruction was going well, nothing frightening

had happened between Crni and me. It turned out that the daunting place I felt compelled to return to over and over again was not the barn, but myself.

Having left a business in the field of health and wellness where I studied eastern and western philosophies and eagerly counseled clients in lifestyle changes, I was beginning to wonder if I had ever put any of this "knowledge" to work in my own life. Was I walking the walk, practicing or merely preaching? Spending time with Crni, I began honing qualities I had always considered admirable, such as patience, persever-

ance, discipline, and intuitive listening. Most importantly, I found that I was being challenged regularly to take stock in myself and my life in ways that were often unsettling but that always resulted in personal growth.

One such lesson occurred as I was riding Crni on a snowy winter afternoon. Bits and pieces of my life had become tangled and messy and I had made no effort to put any of my frustrations aside. As much as my mind was jumbled and dis-

*For horses can educate through first hand,
subjective, personal experiences, unlike
human tutors, teachers and professors
can ever do. Horses can build character, not
merely urge one to improve on it. Horses forge
the mind, the character, the emotions and
inner lives of humans. People can talk to one
another about all these things and remain
distanced and lonesome. In partnership with
a horse, one is seldom lacking for thought,
emotion and inspiration. One is always
attended by a great companion.*

– Charles de Kunffy

tracted it was no wonder Crni seemed agitated as well, which only served to increase my edginess. He finally just refused to move on, planting his feet in a way I construed as defiant instead of interpreting the provocative message he had for me. I raised my riding whip slightly, just enough for him to know it was there, and we were off. Off, that is, out of the arena and bound for a destination I was powerless to control. He wasn't galloping wildly; I did not have the sense that I was in dire danger, but I landed in a snow bank a little shaken.

When I reflected later, I realized some important messages had been sent to me that day. The way I had been handling the problems in my life had been less than thoughtful or even peaceful. I was confusing issues that did not belong together but required separate solutions and attention. I also had to admit that Crni had not dumped me — I had bailed, a very precise metaphor for how I had been living, quitting a little too early and blaming others when I did.

Johann Wolfgang Goethe said, "Thou must learn the thoughts of the noble horse whom thou wouldst ride. The horse is a wise animal. Let him show you the best and most natural way to accomplish a desired end." What the horse truly asks of us is that we be fully alive, awake and present. To genuinely find the freedom that the horse symbolizes takes hard work, determination, honesty, and self-awareness. The reward is reclamation of the self, an enhanced life, and healthier relationships.

There exist countless stories and varying confessions of the unresolved fears and personal triumphs women have discovered under the forgiving and non-judgmental tutelage of the horse. Horses have gained a new prominence as co-facilitators in physical and emotional treatment centers across the nation. Like all animals with which we form a bond, either in our dreams or from a close relationship, horses appear to be catalysts for growth and self-discovery. While I still read lots of instructional books, I prefer to search out the contemporary and historical writings that reinforce my belief that the horse is oracle and bellwether for our souls.

My fondest wish for all girls and women who dream of horses is that they empower themselves with the spirit that is this noble animal. I hope that the thoughts in this book, along with the beautiful photographs and visual images of Mark J. Barrett's DVD, will carry and nurture your imaginations.

AWAKENINGS

If wishes were horses…

Wishes are horses.

*It seems to me we can never give up longing
and wishing while we are thoroughly alive. There
are certain things we feel to be beautiful and good,
and we must hunger after them.*

– George Eliot

Astride a horse as a child, whether a fifty cent ride on a fiberglass image, a rocking horse, or a stick pony, or during a vivid game with friends in the backyard where we gallop wildly in make-believe herds, we become Joan of Arc, Annie Oakley or Pegasus parting the clouds. As children we are large and free to go anywhere our imaginations soar. We may imagine we have hooves instead of bare feet and mighty haunches that propel us, outstretched and full of possibility.

A woman on a horse becomes elevated in powerful proportion to her otherwise two-legged stature. Even as a beginning rider, it is a place of empowerment mixed with the thrill of danger. For many of us this experience opens new doors to adventure, regales the imagination and introduces us to the role of conqueror.

Anaïs Nin wrote, "Dreams pass into the reality of action. From the action stems the dream again; and this interdependence produces the highest form of living." The moment we put one foot in the stirrup and place our bodies and minds horseback, this cycle begins.

A myth is far truer than a history,
for a history only gives a story of the
shadows, whereas a myth gives a story
of the substances that cast the shadows.

– Annie Besant

I add riding to my list of things that look easier than they are!

Innocent beginnings are often startling, often humbling but are always, unequivocally, as joyful as the essence of youth.

When I am new to anything, I am new to the world again no matter my age. With a youthful persistence, I amble forward.

Nothing brings such innocent joy or such a profound awareness that I am not invincible as the horseback experience.

Compassionate human friends, like parents, comfort with words of reassurance, occasionally dusting me off and helping me back into the saddle. The horse himself, of course, is the most provocative of elders. While forgiving, he demands honesty in my ability, testing my forthrightness and diligence.

I am learning bravery and humility. I am discovering fortitude and a stout heart that I didn't know I had.

I shall die very young...
maybe seventy, maybe
eighty, maybe ninety. But I
shall be very young.

– Jeanne Moreau

The longe line between us makes me think of an umbilical cord. It is a preliminary communication line from the ground before I ride on my own. It provides a safer place to be when progressing in the saddle, with my instructor reinforcing me from center circle. At all stages of learning we begin here before the cord is cut.

My horse and I are not just making circles; we are ensphering ourselves in respectful introduction, not only as newcomers but every time we meet. We are finding our balance. We travel in one direction and then the opposite to find weaknesses, and we exercise to correct them. We circuit in close connection to each other to get to know each other, establish contact. We warm up and prepare. We create a centered and ambient energy. I am learning a more delicate and considerate way to form friendships with animals and humans alike.

It is here where I ground myself with reference points. I am looking for "stuck" places and "free" places. I am moving, yet perfecting stillness in my inter-action and my inner-action. I am preparing to breathe on my own.

*Good things are not
done in a hurry.*

– German proverb

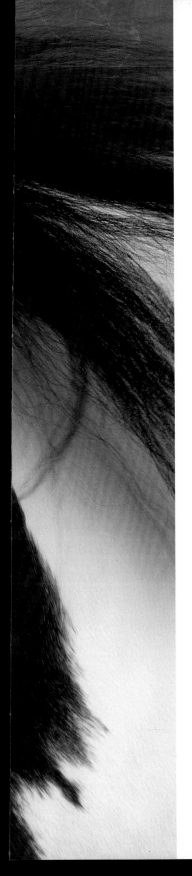

To refine my skills in anything, I need to practice and have patience. Should I expect the horse to immediately bond with me, trust me, perform as I would like? Do I have more than a fragment of information about his world, his temperament or needs? I may set goals, but learning together will not be finished within my human standards of days and calendars, nor should I wish it to be.

Continuous effort —
not strength or intelligence
— is the key to unlocking
our potential.

— Liane Cardes

∩ ∩ ∩ ∩

If one advances confidently
in the direction of his
dreams, and endeavours to
live the life which he has
imagined, he will meet with
a success unexpected in
common hours.

— Henry David Thoreau

Patience and passage of time
do more than strength and fury.

— Jean de la Fontaine

Horsemanship is the one art for which it seems one needs only practice; however, the practice, stripped of sound principles, is nothing more than routine that only results in a forced and uncertain performance and a false brilliance that fascinates the demi-connoisseurs, who are often amazed by the horse's kindness, rather than by the rider's skill.

— Francois Robichon de la Gueriniere

Repeatedly I am asked to regroup, rethink, and to start fresh in accomplishing a task with a horse. Will I ever master the art of horsemanship? Perhaps horsemanship lies in the gift of patience, process and never-ending growth. We will have our "blue ribbon" moments just as all of my efforts in life occasionally award me with accolades, but rewards also reside quietly in the journey.

If I Had A Horse

Something has been excited in my life in this human-equine connection. I am exploring the wonder of anticipation, desire and the magical presence of the horse. At the same time and in equal measure, comfort and complacency have been disturbed. Proceeding in our interrelation means I am coming face to face with some difficult emotions and trials, not the least of which is fear.

Handling a horse from the saddle or the ground can be frightening considering the fact that we are talking about a 1,000 pound plus prey animal with a keen sense of fear herself!

A horse will certainly test you in order to determine who's boss in the relationship. My fear arises when I feel that I lack the self-confidence necessary to be the leader in her world.

Nothing in life is to be feared. It is only to be understood.

— Marie Curie

∩ ∩ ∩ ∩

They are able who think they are able.

— Virgil

Establishing myself as the alpha mare in order for her to feel safe and to accept me in our relationship, I must learn to convey a message of caring authority and also set boundaries that force me to become larger than I am and more powerful in her eyes. I have to stand my ground and move with deliberation, always with assurance and calmness. My authority is seen as nurturance to the horse. Finding that authority nurtures me as well, building my self-esteem. The more time we spend together the more I understand this role, and the more she trusts me.

I accept my fears as a part of life that I need to challenge with reverence and respect with common sense. I am learning to trust my own instincts concerning danger. Through the horse, I have gleaned the freedom and independence to be courageous in the face of faltering.

Life shrinks or expands in
proportion to one's courage.
— Anaïs Nin

Awakenings 35

If I Had A Horse

Being determined, deliberate and decisive, I direct our movements with purpose. I follow through with a plan and am not complacent about my decisions. I must think the action, believe in its purpose, and move with a meaningful carriage.

Women sometimes have a hard time calling the shots, preferring someone else take charge, often accustomed to taking a back seat. Whether we have been conditioned to believe this is our "place" or we have simply never empowered ourselves, the inevitable result is a journey outside an arena, literally or figuratively, and a forfeiture of our voice in the end. Because of my horse experiences, I find myself taking the reins more often in life.

Don't compromise yourself.
You are all you've got.

— Janis Joplin

Faith moves mountains, but you have to keep pushing while you are praying.

— Mason Cooley

∩ ∩ ∩ ∩

Have the courage to act instead of react.

— Earlene Larson Jenks

Awakenings 37

I want to fit in with my peers but I have to be myself. Acceptance by others is more important than it should be sometimes, but I am only trying to find out who I am. I will don many disguises looking for the real me, finding a place in my own herd.

There is a magnet in your heart that will attract true friends…
— Paramahansa Yogananda

Our youth is raw, wild, both fearless and fearful, and fiercely independent while secretly in need of contact. Horses are ageless and non-judgmental companions who teach me responsibility yet help me find my wings. When it is difficult to express my feelings, I'm still okay when I am with horses, all I have to do is just be. I love them and they know it.

Horses change lives. They give our young people confidence and self esteem. They provide peace and tranquility to troubled souls — they give us hope!
— Toni Robinson

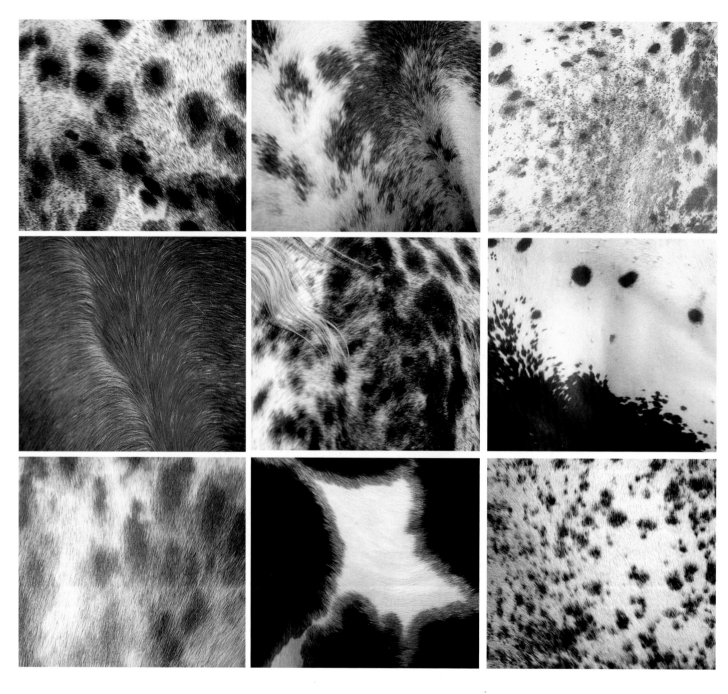

The horse is perfect at being a horse. He has no agenda for tomorrow, no goal to get in shape in time for swimming-suit weather. He knows how to be a horse, perfectly, consummately.

There are a few times when I am lured by magazine images of unattainable physical perfection, and fewer still when I resist my authenticity to conform to what others would have me be. Being with horses teaches me to elaborate on my uniqueness and to fulfill the perfection I was born with because I am accepted in their company as long as I am genuine. This does not entail a model of any body-type or high fashion, just a desire to be real.

Our three horses are as unlike as three persons. Perhaps more so, since they don't read, listen to radio or TV... They don't try to talk like Flicka, walk like Trigger, or eat like Silver.

— Jessamyn West

There is only one success — to be able to spend your life in your own way.

— Christopher Morley

I am not only free to be myself with a horse, I am encouraged to find my brilliance. There may be competition or jealousy among my peers but not between the horse and me. Our relationship thrives the more positive I become about myself. Horses are not envious when we are at our best. Being our best is what they ask of us.

Do not wish to be anything but what you are, and try to be that perfectly.

— St. Francis de Sales

∩ ∩ ∩ ∩

My great mistake, the fault for which I can't forgive myself is that one day I ceased my obstinate pursuit of my own individuality.

— Oscar Wilde

44 If I Had A Horse

R econnected to the earth…

When the bitter winds howl and cut through layers of cloth-
ing, and fingers and toes go numb from cold, or when the sun
beats skin to parchment after having pared down to the
necessities of attire, brimmed hat shielding face, sealed in fly
spray, perspiration running down my back — there is a satis-
faction that comes from facing the elements with a horse.
Muddy, smudged, grime beneath nails, real and earthy fra-
grances of horse, barn, myself — all rejuvenate and serve as
reminders of who I really am undisguised by perfume or coif-
feur. I am a woman close to the earth.

Bathing later has new meaning as it eases the muscles and regulates body temperature, but my
cleansing has already occurred. I emerge and tie
wet hair close to my head, tend to insect bites or
dry skin, omit all masks and revel in the day.

I sweat. If anything comes
easy to me, I mistrust it.
— Lilli Palmer

∩ ∩ ∩ ∩

We are of the earth, made of the same stuff;
there is no other, no division between us
and the "lower" or "higher" forms of being.
— Estella Lauder

The horse and I will have moments of triumph, bursting with thrill and accomplishment. Whether or not we choose to compete, riding is a sport and our achievements last beyond the experience and build assurance. The essence of these moments provides the kind of truthful self-confidence that radiates in all of life. Recognizable by all, this elation, however, remains faithfully personal.

Confidence is a plant of slow growth.

— Anna Leonowens

∩ ∩ ∩ ∩

One never believes other people's experience, and one is only very gradually convinced by one's own.

— Vita Sackville-West

Confidence starts in the mind, blossoms in action, and grows with practice. In the culmination of encounters that naturally build certitude in my capabilities, I allow myself the recognition of what I have accomplished.

I raise my hands in the air, smile for the world to see, shout myself to the wind! But I do so without arrogance, for this is mine alone and may encompass another's greatest fear.

Conserving the experiences that challenge, I do all I can to build on them. Even if I fall short, I have had the courage to try. I remember those who have encouraged me and I admire the prancing horse, my partner.

There is an applause superior to that of the multitude — one's own.

— Elizabeth Elton Smith

Horses afford us the luxury of enchantment. While there may be no romancing boarding fees and vet bills, whenever a horse emerges in your life, fantasy awakens. Horses fuel the imaginations of children and nurture the youthful souls of adults.

I feel a connection to the fabled stories of women and horses the more time I spend in a horse's company. Every mare, stallion or gelding has a tale to tell and a symbolism that enriches our lives. I am revisiting the classics from mythology to fairy tales and finding new meaning. Often in my dreams our journeys are fantastic and surreal, but these same dreams are linked to the awakening of an enchantment that was in danger of being lost. I look at the world a little differently now, with more wonder.

The most beautiful thing we can experience is the mysterious. It is the source of all true art and science.

— Albert Einstein

We are spirit, the horse and I... vital and animated, essence and substance, specter and apparition, boldness, enthusiasm and ardor.

We are sprites, the horse and I... mythological figures empowered with magical gifts and the stuff of childhood tales. Often diaphanous or forced to be in the shadows, we appear with deliberate intent when messages need to be delivered.

We all hunger for the enigmatic, the veiled unexplainable which is beyond human understanding. Some of us satisfy this appetite with the archetypal majesty and power of the horse.

Courage, wisdom born of insight and humility, empathy born of compassion and love, all can be bequeathed by a horse to his rider.

— Charles de Kunffy

If I Had A Horse

52   *If I Had A Horse*

TRANSITIONS

*There is no way in which to understand
the world without first detecting it
through the radar-net of our senses.*

— Diane Ackerman

If I Had A Horse

Horses are highly alert creatures, responding to our touch, smell, changes in respiration and heart rate. For as long as they have inhabited the earth, horses have relied on acute senses for survival. Horses depend on subtle messages from their environment and from other animals, including humans, for signs of comfort or alarm.

Our time together reminds me that I am a sensory being too, open to a world of subtle messages where listening is not always auditory communication. I am becoming more sensitive to the innate instincts of our natural world, and more compassionate to other living beings.

I am exploring the ability we all have for a language without linguistics. Dormant for most of us today, this ability is further diminished when we are disconnected from animals and nature in general.

If you atrophy one sense you also atrophy all the others, a sensuous and physical connection with nature, with art, with food, with other human beings.

— Anaïs Nin

If I Had A Horse

If I Had A Horse

"Think trot," suggests my instructor as the horse walks on. I do, with concentration. The horse trots.

Have I accomplished this command with my mind alone? When I put my mind to the word, the thought manifests in signals in my body, the energy kicks up, imperceptible to all but the horse. He is skilled in hearing the cues that I must practice to communicate. I find it amazing that he understands me, despite its naturalness.

When I feel as though I no longer have a horse's attention, I focus on myself. Struggling in a place between our worlds where words lie at the bottom of our communication resources, I utilize the language of feel, timing, balance, and mental concentration.

In a perfect trot, balanced and rhythmic, this horse moves while remaining connected to me. I breathe slowly and deeply and think, "Shhhhh, walk." He walks.

An understanding of a horse's nature is one of the first basics in the art of riding, and all horsemen must make this their principle consideration.

— Francois Robichon de la Gueriniere

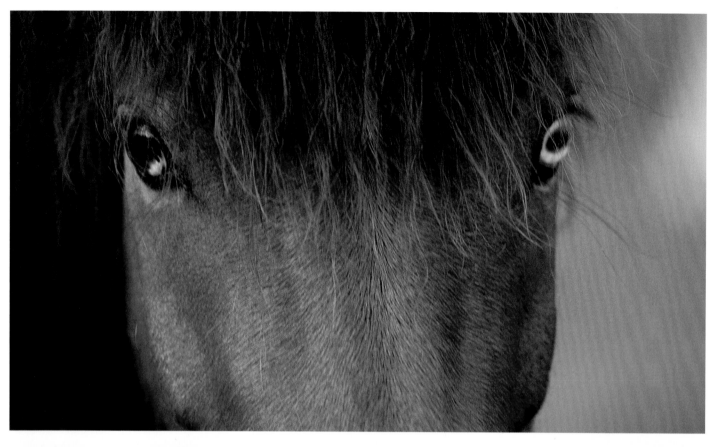

Communicating with a horse requires a sensitivity that I find helpful in my human relationships. Gestures, facial expressions, words unspoken yet conveyed in body language, have become more obvious to me, and I revere them as profound communication tools. I find I am a better listener. Acutely aware of the influence my thoughts have on those around me, I am a more positive person.

There are many times that the only way I am able to understand a horse, is to think like a horse. I feel as if she understands my empathy, or perhaps just appreciates the time I am willing to devote to her world. After all, any worthwhile friendship has, at its core, honor and mutual respect. Because of these horse experiences, I find it easier to walk in another's shoes.

Between whom there is a hearty truth, there is love.

— Henry David Thoreau

Once a human being has arrived on this earth, communication is the largest single factor determining what kinds of relationships he makes with others and what happens to him in the world about him.

— Virginia Satir

Of course, the horse and I do have a few verbal understandings. I know a contented whinny or the sound of a stress releasing snort or yawn. I have experienced the ear-piercing pitch of a call from a horse to his herd mates. I can usually elicit a response when I say, "Whoa" or "Back," and most especially, "Good boy."

There is also the universal "cluck." Not to be used lightly, it nevertheless is an indispensable tool in communicating action of one kind or another to the horse. Exclusive to the horse and human, practicing the cluck in public may get you strange looks. It also fails to speed up long lines in the super-market or, if performed twice in rapid succession, may be construed as flirting. Clucking will also not help to move large pieces of obstinate furniture that will not budge when you are trying to back them up or move them forward!

If I Had A Horse

Music becomes another bridge between the horse and human worlds. Listening to music with a horse calms or energizes the atmosphere and creates correspondence. Transmissions of sound, like touch, have the power to soothe in a stressful situation or to rev up the pace in a workout. Music composes us while drawing attention to a message. The message is one we often share.

Music gives access to regions in the subconscious that can be reached in no other way.

— Sophie Drinker

∩ ∩ ∩ ∩

Notes fly so much farther than words. There is no other way to reach the infinite.

— Anaïs Nin

∩ ∩ ∩ ∩

Music is the shorthand of emotion.

— Leo Tolstoy

∩ ∩ ∩ ∩

After silence, that which comes nearest to expressing the inexpressible is music.

— Aldous Huxley

R hythms and beats in life become the gaits of horses. The patterns of sounds around me evoke a steady walk, a collected trot, a rolling three beat canter.

Forever choreographing in daydreams whenever music stirred me, my visions have changed to the percussion of hooves and of rolling muscles lifting and pushing in cadenced performances together. We are dance partners even when we are apart.

Life's energy is stirred in a need to dance, to let go. Remembering this I will find my rhythm and let the movement of the horse limber and supple my body. I will dance with a new swing in my hips.

The body has its own way of knowing,
a knowing that has little to do with logic,
and much to do with truth, little to do with
control, and much to do with acceptance,
little to do with division and analysis,
and much to do with union.
— Marilyn Sewell

*Dance is the hidden
language of the soul.*
— Martha Graham

If I Had A Horse

I am coming to terms with a simple fact: As soon as you think things are certain, they certainly are not.

Nothing stays the same. Tests and setbacks always accompany victories and successes. Challenges give the horse and I opportunities to know each other better so that we may act in unison to hurdle the roadblocks, even though yesterday they did not exist and tomorrow there may be new ones. Praise becomes more important in even the smallest moments of progression and grace starts to replace frustration.

Comfort can be found in change. When everything falls apart something is to be gained. With high aspirations comes the realization that lessons never end. Adaptability allows alternatives in problem solving and shows the possibility of open routes to a goal. Because of the horse in my life, I consider the means to an end and keep an open mind towards all the avenues available. Bumps in the road don't throw me off.

If the angel deigns to come, it will be because you have convinced him, not by tears, but by your humble resolve to be always beginning: to be a beginner.
— Rainer Maria Rilke

Do I contradict myself?
Very well then I contradict myself.
(I am large, I contain multitudes.)
— Walt Whitman

∩ ∩ ∩ ∩

Problems are messages.
— Shakti Gawain

"Keep moving forward!" the riding instructor demands. The horse and I are no longer on the same wavelength and things are deteriorating rapidly. Continuing on is one of the hardest things to do when things are coming apart.

What I am finding, however, is the miraculous power of forward moving and thinking. When I resist the urge to halt and instead put diligence to the test, issues work themselves out with less interference than imagined. When everything finally comes together harmoniously on the back of a horse, if only for a moment, it feels like magic.

This is the same momentum necessary to move out of any of life's challenges. Futility is now reserved in my life only for expenditures that are not of a worthy cause. Otherwise, quitting is not in my vocabulary. I repeat "go forward, be round" and roll ahead.

*When you get in a tight place and
everything goes against you till
it seems as though you could not
hold on a minute longer, never give
up then, for that is just the time
and the place the tide will turn.*
— Harriet Beecher Stowe

The visualization and centeredness that I am acquiring through riding helps me prepare for any test life hands me.

I am concentrating on the here and now. While the horse is the perfect metaphor for movement and forward thinking, each moment spent in our communion requires complete awareness of the present. I become focused on one thing alone.

With the horse, I am encased in a world finely tuned to reciprocal communication where there is no room for thoughts of yesterday or tomorrow. Surroundings do not disappear but become integrated and acknowledged as we concentrate on moving together, engaging in a mutual meditation, in mantras of intentional presence.

Liberated from all else and focused solely on the process at hand, the riding hours in life afford the opportunity to savor the present. Breathing and movement are in symmetry and worries fade for a while. I become a creature moving on four legs.

When I dance, I dance; when I sleep, I sleep: Yes, and when I am walking by myself in a beautiful orchard, even if my thoughts dwell for part of the time on distant events, I bring them back for another part to the walk, the orchard, the charm of this solitude, and to myself. Nature has with maternal care provided that the actions she has enjoined on us for our need shall give us pleasure; and she uses not only reason but appetite to attract us to them. It is wrong to infringe her rules.

— Michel De Montaigne

There are times when I just need to let things be. When I become absorbed in analysis, dissecting each fragment of my aids, the horse's gait, why this worked and why that didn't, my furrowed brow reveals an over-active mind. I have forgotten to relax.

There have been moments horseback, however fleeting, when I have been afforded *bliss*. There is no other word to explain it. It occurs when I have given up the how and why, where I feel as though I am doing nothing and everything at the same time.

What we seek we do not find — that would be too trim and tidy for so reckless and opulent a thing as life. It is something else we find.

— Susan Glaspell

∩ ∩ ∩ ∩

Analysis kills spontaneity. The grain once ground into flour springs and germinates no more.

— Henri Frederic Amiel

∩ ∩ ∩ ∩

It is not a question of analyzing yourself. It is a question of seeing yourself.

— Yogaswami

I struggle to find the best way to describe this feeling, but I am seldom successful unless I am speaking to another who has experienced what I am trying to convey and who nods in acknowledgement, unable to put the phenomenon in any better words herself, and who is grateful for a comrade. It is a risky experience to share, reserved for confidences amongst the most trusted friends or family.

That "thing" I have found on a horse and strive so hard to duplicate will never be found as long as I am searching for it, but will present itself, occasionally, when I have forgotten about it... gotten out if its way. I am discovering that being a student in relationship to a horse does not entail the dogmatic. It is a far more organic experience.

If I Had A Horse

Horses have redefined surrender for me. I no longer think of surrender as a forfeiture of will or power. It is not the submissive act I once deemed it to be but the wondrous relinquishment of unnecessary restrictions that keep me from true enjoyment. I am finding freedom in abandonment and marveling in the ease that I feel from a horse when we let all else go and move together comfortably.

When you have entirely surrendered,
everything you do will be meditation.

— Yogaswami

Monotony is the law of nature. Look at the monotonous manner in which the sun rises. The monotony of necessary occupations is exhilarating and life-giving.

— Gandhi

Routines are healthy; keeping things fresh is the key. Mindfully methodical, I am open to the benefits of ritual and aware of the slightest opportunity for progression. Much of life follows a pattern that I often long to break until I find the blessings in the doing. Paying attention during the mundane is a realization that there need never be a moment that is ordinary or ever quite the same as the last. My senses are on fire after time spent with a horse, no matter what tasks confront me.

The strength of a man's virtue should not be measured by his special exertions, but by his habitual acts.

– Blaise Pascal

∩ ∩ ∩ ∩

There is no enlightenment outside of daily life.

— Thich Nhat Hanh

84 *If I Had A Horse*

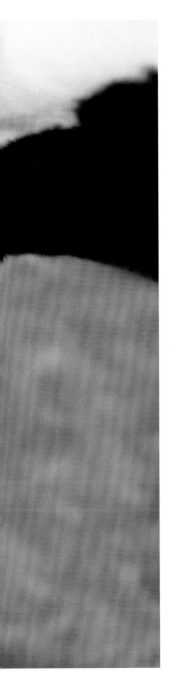

Horses are experts at mirroring the truth of who we are and what we are feeling. If I am anxious and stressed and put on a false face, she immediately identifies what I am trying to disguise. The softness that I know she possesses is replaced with a tossing head and a wary eye. I am pretending to be peaceful and she knows it.

The finest teachers stretch our worlds and pique our interests in places where we never thought to delve. As finely as the horse mirrors my true self, I have no choice if I am to be in her company but to recognize myself. Instead of trying to shed my skin and falsify claims, I now try to transform and let go of what I need to eliminate emotionally.

In our company, a horse's behavior reveals more about who we are than who they are. I am becoming more honest about my feelings and less ashamed of them. There have been times I have buried my head in the sweet smell of a horse's neck while tears flowed easily. The horse, this teacher, has expanded then released her sides as she let out a long, rippling snort.

It takes two to speak the truth — one to speak, and another to hear.

— Henry David Thoreau

∩ ∩ ∩ ∩

He who knows others is wise; He who knows himself is enlightened.

— Lao-Tzu

In middle age, horses open opportunities in the face of transition.

Instead of thinking of this point in life as a crisis, I find a place of freedom. In the prime of life, while perhaps at the height of responsibilities, I find myself paring down to essentials. It is precisely at this elusive time that I find an opportunity to flourish and blossom. Through the new experience of journeying horseback, women find themselves on a maiden voyage with the knowledge of a seasoned traveler.

Perhaps middle age is, or should be,
a period of shedding shells; the shell of
ambition, the shell of material accumulations and
possessions, the shell of the ego.

— Anne Morrow Lindbergh

When one door of happiness closes,
another opens; but often we look so
long at the closed door that we do not
see the one which has been opened for us.

— Helen Keller

∩ ∩ ∩ ∩

Make voyages. Attempt them.
There's nothing else.

— Tennessee Williams

If I Had A Horse

It is important for women to follow their desires and to make time for themselves. I refuse to be dissuaded from my instinctual knowledge that my own growth is essential to all whom I care for, and to my own worth.

A horse has captured my imagination. It is a worthwhile occurrence, a medicinal experience that sends ripples of itself into everything else I do, to everything and everyone that I love.

Women aren't trying to do too much. Women have too much to do.

— Mary Kay Blakely

∩ ∩ ∩ ∩

Woman's normal occupations in general run counter to creative life, or contemplative life, or saintly life.

— Anne Morrow Lindbergh

∩ ∩ ∩ ∩

Time, when it is left to itself and no definite demands are made on it, cannot be trusted to move at any recognized pace. Usually it loiters; but just when one has come to count upon its slowness, it may suddenly break into a wild irrational gallop.

— Edith Wharton

There is always a reason a horse appears in a woman's life. It is no accident when they come to us, if only in our dreams. If our hearts fill with longing thinking of them, they carry a potent message. Horses may enter our lives for a short time or be present throughout. However they make a presence, their impact is permanent. Carrying us at crossroads, assisting us with burdens, empowering us with sensations of flight and freedom, they often catch us off guard with the possibility of new horizons and secret gates to our souls that need unlocking.

If I Had A Horse

TRANSFORMATIONS

To perceive the truth, there must be
a focusing of attention. This does not mean
turning away from distraction. There is no such
thing as distraction, because life is a movement
and has to be understood as a total process.

— Krishnamurti

If I Had A Horse

Times when I am mired in the complexities of modern life are times when I lose so many precious moments. When I feel misplaced, unable to just be, and I am searching for ways to be at peace, all I need is a trip to the barn to reconnect me to simplicity.

Here I find a simple grace in being alive and interacting with my senses. We go for a ride and everything that is outside of this landscape begins to take a back seat. I begin to think of being sensitive in a new way, in a more natural and less complicated existence. The things that I wish to truly affect my life are here. This reality is the one that allows me to be an available human being.

It was on that road and at that hour
that I first became aware of my own self,
experienced an inexpressible state of grace,
and felt one with the first breath of air
that stirred, the first bird,
and the sun so newly born
that it still looked not quite round."

– Colette

Transformations   99

Solace and serenity are mine throughout the day as I recall early mornings, soft, beckoning whinnies, the sound of my lone footsteps passing the stalls, and the sweet smell of horse and hay. We commune as he gathers me in, stretching to nuzzle closer to my scent, in recognition of my presence, my voice, in this quiet time. There is this special place to return to when the world is not so still; it lives with me always.

Whatever peace I know rests in the natural world,
in feeling myself a part of it, even in a small way.

– May Sarton

I have always been a
lover of tranquility
And when I see this
clear stream so
Calm
I want to stay on some
great rock
And fish for ever and
ever on.

— Wang Wei

It is quite apparent that horses have a lot to teach us about the sanctity of idle hours and energy conservation! Chances are they are just eating and relaxing, not worrying about wasting time or thinking of things they should be doing instead. I leave some things undone these days, making better use of my time by just watching horses "be" for a while.

There is no pleasure in having nothing to do; the fun is in having lots to do — and not doing it.

— Mary Wilson Little

Thanks to the horse, I have a new found sense of humor. It comes from taking myself less seriously. Remarkably, the complexities of learning to ride promptly eased up the minute I relaxed a bit and found the amusement in my shortcomings.

I certainly have to smile and laugh a bit now whenever faced with a challenge. Horses are no strangers to humor. They are often the most playful and clever of comics, having impeccable timing!

One is healthy when one can laugh at the earnestness and zeal with which one has been hypnotized by any single detail on one's life.

— Friedrich Nietzsche

He deserves paradise who makes his companions laugh.

— The Koran

∩ ∩ ∩ ∩

Humor comes from self-confidence. There's an aggressive element to wit.

– Rita Mae Brown

If I Had A Horse

Balance, that equality of distribution between excess and deficiency, can be so elusive. Stability requires constant attention to harmony and equilibrium. Readjustments in life are necessary but knee-jerk reactions to sudden imbalances, while human nature, solve little and throw everyone else off balance as well.

It takes a certain amount of grace and a lot of practice to truly be in balance. Achieving balance on a horse takes physical and mental acuity. When poised, there is a dignity to our manner, a composure that we all admire. We have to earn that kind of composure, and it is a feat, considering all of the unpredictable occurrences in life.

Grace is so great an adornment for a rider, and at the same time so important a means to the knowledge of all that which is necessary for persons aspiring to become riders, that such persons should willingly spend the time required to obtain that quality at the outside of their endeavours."

— Francois Robichon de la Gueriniere

*Friend, our closeness
is this: anywhere you
put your foot, feel me
in the firmness
under you.*

– Rumi

∩ ∩ ∩ ∩

*Trust, which is a virtue,
is also a habit, like prayer.
It requires exercise.
And just as no one
can run five miles a day
and cede the cardiovascular
effects to someone else,
no one can trust for us.*

– Sue Halpern

y feet are far from the ground. I am on an animal
hurdling through space. I must find my own
confidence and convey an ease to this partner. She needs
my assurance as surely as I need hers. We are different
creatures on our own. Here, we need faith in each other
to comfortably move on.

Consigning confidence in each other places trust in a tight
circle of dependency, but still allows for times when we are
less than assured. There are elements beyond our confines
that may threaten, but faith in each other, confidence in ourselves and most importantly, time together, provide the
groundwork (how important groundwork is!) for trust. It is
no different in any of my relationships.

If I Had A Horse

Anger has a purpose and a place — outside of my time with a horse. Anger is as necessary for survival as any emotion. It is not always the adversarial flame that we have been taught, but the legitimate prerogative of all creatures of both genders. Anger is unhealthy, like all of the emotions, only when it is suppressed or when it is excessive, unresolved.

Anger excites a passion that protests for our rights, that claims boundaries. If it is direct, to the point, it serves by giving us information about our feelings of self-worth or of the protection of the principles that we hold dear. Sometimes, like love, anger is the only driving force against what would otherwise become fear. It is reasonable to put your foot down when the fundamental privileges we are all entitled to are infringed upon. Sometimes you have to put your foot down to get a leg up.

I have become aware of what it means to hold reins connected to a metal bar in a horse's mouth, of my weight on his back and of my lack of awareness at times of his fine temperament and good will. He has shown me anger in sudden little bucks, unwillingness to move, or pinned ears and flashing eyes. I am apologetic and grateful for his forgiving nature. I am no longer ashamed of my own bucks and flashes.

Anger as soon as fed is dead —
'Tis starving makes it fat.

— Emily Dickinson

Considering what we ask of a horse, kindness becomes a way of selfless giving. Horses who have been treated unkindly will quickly teach you the magnitude of unsympathetic care. Like all sentient creatures, she may be withdrawn and impassible or agitated and hypersensitive.

I have found that all animals (and most humans) who are respected and treated with kindness, barring any physiological or psychological barrier, will respond with their hearts. Horses, moreover, have a special dignity that requires authenticity from us. If we are not genuine in our care and kindness towards them, they sense the manipulative nature of our actions.

There is a certain consideration,
and a general duty of humanity,
that binds us not only to the animals,
which have life and feeling, but
even to the trees and plants.
We owe justice to men, and kindness
and benevolence to all other creatures
who may be susceptible of it.
There is some intercourse between
them and us, and some
mutual obligation.

– Michel De Montaigne

The horse has taught me that kindness, in its highest form, must be disengaged from self-gain. If altruism had a perfect manifestation, it might be kindness.

I prefer you make mistakes in kindness
than work miracles in unkindness.

— Mother Teresa

∩ ∩ ∩ ∩

A brave man is seldom unkind.

— Pretty-Shield, Medicine Woman

If I Had A Horse

The photographer captures the perfect moment, a piece of time stolen and frozen on film. The painter brushes form and shadow onto a canvas. The writer infuses the reading mind with images, using meticulously chosen words. Dancers, composers, performers… all surrender themselves to the passion of self and to the impassioned interpretation of others.

Horses and the creativity that they instill have moved me to become an artist of sorts. I am inspired by them to find the hidden element that harmonizes with their aesthetic beauty, to feel over and over again the perfection in the evanescent moments on a horse when life is a flash of art.

What was any art but an effort to make a sheath, a mold in which to imprison for a moment the shining, elusive element which is life itself,–life hurrying past us and running away, too strong to stop, too sweet to lose?

– Willa Cather

To create one's own world in any of the arts takes courage.

– Georgia O'Keefe

∩ ∩ ∩ ∩

The artist is not a special kind of person; rather each person is a special kind of artist.

– Ananda Coomaraswamy

I am wild by nature.

There remains the untamable nature of the horse, at his core. It is at once intimidating and romantically wild. That is surely part of why I ride, to provoke the wildness in myself.

If you have got a living force and you're not using it, nature kicks you back. The blood boils just like you put it in a pot.

— Louise Nevelson

I am not afraid of the inherent nature of the horse any more than I am compelled to tame my own instinctual behavior. I am wary of any attempt to do away with this quality. There are times when we both need to be unbridled, unharnessed, and undomesticated.

I do not desire to be "broken" to the point of mere slavery any more that the horse does. Any attempt to fracture my integral freedom will certainly result in as unwilling a partner as any horse who has been disrespected in this way. Whomever holds the tether is likewise tied and as unlikely to soar.

The world never puts a price on you higher than the one you put on yourself.

— Sonja Henie

My connection to animals has grown the more I realize we are not separate.

The cat exchanges her aloofness for attention, burying her head in my hand for a stroke, precisely when I am feeling lonely. The dog sits on my feet as I cry, comforting the best way he can at the moment, and succeeding. The horse lowers his towering head as I rub his ears. We are eye to eye for what seems like eternity. Infinity is exactly what I see, saecula saeculorum, forever and a day. I feel new again, yet old and imperishable in my soul.

It is not that we have a soul, we are a soul.

– Amelia E. Barr

I think everything and everyone slept that afternoon in Little Rock. I sat with my dog in a cool place on the north side of my grandparents' clapboard home. Hydrangeas flourished there, shaded from the heat. The domed blue flowers were higher than our heads. I held the dog's head, stroking her into sleep. But she held my gaze. As I looked into her eyes I realized that I would never travel further than into this animal's eyes. At this particular moment I was allowed to see infinity through my dog's eyes, and I was old enough to know that. They were as deep, as bewildering, as unattainable as a night sky.

– Meinrad Craighead

My spirit has found an open window, the myth of the horse experienced.

What I knew of myself has been eclipsed on horseback. This has occurred without my summoning and without warning. There is some physical peace that precedes it, I know that much, where my body is effortlessly floating on the back of another effortlessly moving creature. Suddenly there are no thoughts and time is meaningless.

Just at this place, an essence of myself is vividly present. It has no nameable form, for it is all forms, and like the great shadow of an eclipse, it hides the familiarity that I have of myself and opens a window for my soul. For what is probably only an instant, I am nothing but spirit.

My thoughts return and I savor the wonder. Have I just been afforded a hint, a glimpse of truth? I only smile, for there is nothing else to do, except to recall as best I can, and as often as I am able, a simple yet powerful knowledge of connectedness.

∩ ∩ ∩ ∩

Those things that nature denied to human sight,
she revealed to the eyes of the soul.

– Ovid

Our spirit is a being of nature quite
indestructible and its activity continues
from eternity to eternity. It is like the sun,
which seems to set only to our earthly eyes,
but which, in reality, never sets,
but shines on unceasingly.

— J.W. von Goethe

If I Had A Horse

Horses will always run through my bloodstream. Perhaps I have been fortunate enough in my lifetime to live where the landscape included horses, where pasture and barn spread from my picture windows. Perhaps I have lived borrowing slips of time with horses, seizing the opportunity to be with them whenever possible. Maybe I have only lived with horses in special places in my heart and mind alone, a place I could always visit, where the horse and I soared, empowering my imagination and self-ownership. Our hearts, after all, hold landscapes and realities far broader than the eye can see.

I have wisdom to impart and a collection of glorious stories to tell. My granddaughters sit at my feet spellbound. They hold porcelain horses in their hands.

Time and trouble will tame an advanced young woman. But an advanced old woman is uncontrollable by any force.

— Dorothy L. Sayers

∩ ∩ ∩ ∩

When I can't ride anymore, I shall keep horses as long as I can hobble along with a bucket and wheelbarrow. When I can't hobble, I shall roll my wheelchair out by the fence of the field where my horses graze, and watch them.

— Monica Dickens

In mythology animals are recognized for the endowment of their special gifts. There was a time when we weren't concerned about whether or not this was "anthropomorphizing."

When the genuine myth rises into consciousness, that is always its message. You must change your life.

–Ursula K. Le Guin

Could it be, that the horse as messenger, is such a profound teacher because once upon a time when we listened to all healers, all creatures who, in one way or another, inspired us to remember what we already knew, the horse persuaded us to believe in ourselves?

As long as we do not ask the horse to forget who he is, he will remind us of who we want to be.

That's what learning is. You suddenly understand something you understood your whole life, but in a new way.

— Doris Lessing

If I Had A Horse

If I Had A Horse

SOURCES

Grateful acknowledgment is made to the authors and publishers for use of the following material. If notified, the publisher will be pleased to rectify an omission in future editions.

Ackerman, Diane. *A Natural History of the Senses.* New York: Random House, 1990.

Allen, Paula Gunn. *The Sacred Hoop: Recovering the Feminine in American Indian Traditions.* Boston: Beacon Press, 1986.

Blakely, Mary Kay. *American Mom: Motherhood, Politics, and Humble Pie.* Chapel Hill, NC: Algonquin Books of Chapel Hill, 1994.

Brown, Rita Mae. *Starting From Scratch: A Different Kind of Writer's Manual.* Toronto; New York: Bantam Books, 1988.

Craighead, Meinrad. *The Mother's Song: Images of God the Mother.* New York: Paulist Press, 1986.

Drinker, Sophie. *Music and Women: The Story of Women in Their Relation to Music.* New York: The Feminist Press a the City University of New York, 1995.

Gawain, Shakti. *Living in the Light: A Guide to Personal and Planetary Transformations.* Novato, CA: New World Library, 1998.

Gueriniere, Robichon de la. *Ecole De Cavalerie.* Xenophon Press, 1992. Translation from French copyright © 1978 & 1979 by EDA Corp.

Halpern, Sue. *Migrations to Solitude.* New York: Vintage Books, 1993.

Jenks, Earlene Larson. *Go For The Gold: Thoughts on Achieving Your Personal Best.* Kansas City, MO: Andrews and McMeel, 1995.

Kunffy, Charles de. *The Ethics and Passions of Dressage.* Middletown, MD: Half Halt Press, 1993.

Lindbergh, Anne Morrow. *Gift From The Sea.* New York: Pantheon, 1955.

Morgan, Susan (Edit.). *The Romance of the Harem.* Charlottesville: University Press of Virginia, 1991.

Oliveira, Nuno. *Notes and Reminiscences of a Portuguese Rider.* London: J.A. Allen, 1976.

Paupst, James C. and Toni Robinson. *Breakdown or Breakthrough: Self-Discovery Through Change.* Agincourt, Ont: Gage Publishing, 1980.

Riley, Glenda. *Women and Nature: Saving the "Wild West."* Lincoln, NB: University of Nebraska Press, 1999.

Sarton, May. *Journal of Solitude.* New York: Norton, 1973.

Satir, Virginia. *Peoplemaking.* Palo Alto: California Science and Behavior Books, 1972.

Sewell, Marilyn. *Cries of the Spirit: A Celebration of Women's Spirituality.* Boston: Beacon Press, 1991.

Sitwell, Edith. *Taken Care Of: The Autobiography of Edith Sitwell.* New York: Atheneum, 1965.

Walker, Alice. *Living By The Word: Selected Writings 1973-1987.* San Diego: Harcourt Brace Jovanovich, 1988.